When the Kingdom Comes

DAILY READINGS FOR ADVENT FROM ISAIAH

D1739233

CARRE COY PHILLIPS

When The Kingdom Comes: Daily Readings for Advent from Isaiah
Copyright © 2023 by Carre Coy Phillips

Scripture quotations are from The ESV® Bible (The Holy Bible, English
Standard Version®), copyright © 2001 by Crossway, a publishing
ministry of Good News Publishers. Used by permission.
All rights reserved.
All italics and bold fonts in quotations of Scripture have been added by
the authors.
Original artwork by Elsbeth DeRuischer
Art digitalization by Hannah Moody
Cover and layout design by Lauren Rives
Edited by Beth Joseph, MDiv

ISBN: 9798862057850
Imprint: Independently published

Library of Congress Cataloging-in-Publication Data is on file at the
Library of Congress, Washington, DC

This book is dedicated to the ones who believed
in me and this message from the very beginning.

To Andrew, my best friend and my biggest champion,
you sacrificed many days and nights to see these
pages come to life. Thank you for listening,
processing, and championing this story of hope.

And to my dear girlfriends, who believe Jesus can do
extraordinary things through ordinary people like me.
I am eternally grateful for your pursuit of the kingdom
and your willingness to speak life into me. Your words of
encouragement are scattered across the pages of this book.

For to us a child is born,

to us a son is given;

and the government shall

be upon his shoulder,

and his name shall be called

Wonderful Counselor, Mighty God, Everlasting Father, Prince of Peace.

ISAIAH 9:6

Table of Contents

Dear friends,

With the greatest joy and excitement, I invite you into this Advent season. For thousands of years, the Church has been slowing down for Advent to remember the birth of Jesus. Christmas is all about Jesus. The long-awaited Messiah came to bring His kingdom to earth.

December can be one of the most chaotic times of the year. The Christmas season can quickly fill up with parties, shopping, decorating, and travel. It's easy to get lost in the busyness of Christmas and forget what it's all about.

When I first had the idea to write an Advent study, I began reading other books previously written. I began to notice there were great daily devotionals and Bible studies, but there weren't many daily reading plans based on a specific book of the Bible. As much as I love to sit down and study the Bible, I recognize that for many of us, December tends to be one of the busiest months of the year. I hope this book will equip you with quick daily readings and reflections to focus on our living hope during your Christmas celebrations.

For the daily reading plan, I purposefully chose to study Isaiah. With select readings from across the book, we look back at God's people, the Israelites, who were awaiting someone to rescue them. In the first advent, they were waiting for the arrival of Jesus Christ—the Messiah. This season, we can celebrate God's fulfillment of that promise! As we also wait for the second advent, I hope these pages will stir in you a more profound longing for Jesus, our Messiah.

In this Christmas season, let's slow down and behold our Savior. Together, may we find fresh hope by remembering His faithfulness and promises for *our* future when Jesus returns to fully bring His kingdom to earth.

Merry Christmas,

Carre

Carre Coy Phillips

Isaiah was a prophet.

Prophets were messengers who brought a word from God to the people.

THE BACKGROUND

Outside of God, Isaiah is the predominant voice and prophet in the book of Isaiah. While there is some scholarly debate on who wrote the futuristic prophecies from the exile in Babylon, Isaiah is the only known author of this book.

Isaiah was married to a prophetess with two sons. He received his call to prophetic ministry in the year that King Uzziah died (740 BC). Isaiah lived in Jerusalem, the capital city of Judah. Because of his easy access to the kings and their court, Isaiah may have had some association or lineage with the royal bloodline. Whatever the connection might have been, it allowed him an opportunity to reach the entire nation of Judah by his associations.

Although there is no official historical record of his death, Jewish scholars hold that Isaiah was martyred under the reign of King Manasseh because of his prophesying.

THE LOCATION

Kingdom: Judah
Capital: Jerusalem
People: Israelites
Other Names: Zion is both a nickname for the city of Jerusalem and the future dwelling place of God.

THE MESSAGE

The book of Isaiah is built around three portraits of the coming Messiah:
- King
- Servant
- Anointed Conqueror

Timeline

Isaiah's ministry spanned the following kings:

KING UZZIAH

740/39 BC

KING JOTHAM

732/31 BC

KING AHAZ

716/15 BC

KING HEZEKIAH

687/86 BC

Advent

stems from a Latin word that means "coming" or "arrival."

For Christians throughout the world, Advent refers to the four weeks leading up to Christmas, where communities remember and celebrate the arrival of Jesus and join together in the hope of His ultimate return.

The purpose of Advent is to help believers remain focused on Christ during the Christmas season. We retell the story of the first advent to awaken hope for the promise of the second advent.

How To Use These Daily Readings

Read the daily passage in a Bible of your choice.*

Read the devotion that goes with the passage.

Spend some time looking back at the Scripture passage.
Consider these questions:

What does this reveal to us about God?

What verse or words stand out to you in a fresh way?

How does this make you long for the second advent?

Spend some time in prayer, slowing down to talk with God about what you're reading. Ask Him to give you a fresh desire to focus on eternal things.

* To encourage you to actually open and read your Bible, only one key verse is included each day. While it's possible to only read this verse, reading the entire daily passage will help you stay rooted in God's Word and provide better context for your daily readings.

He shall judge between the nations, and shall decide disputes for many peoples; and they shall beat their swords into plowshares, and their spears into pruning hooks; nation shall not lift up sword against nation, neither shall they learn war anymore.

ISAIAH 2:4

The Light of the World Has Come

In the beginning, God walked with Adam and Eve in the Garden of Eden. The garden was alive and flourishing. Everything existed perfectly, with the wildlife roaming, the trees blooming, and the river flowing. Yet tragically, as we know, Adam and Eve sinned, and the world has been in chaos ever since.

Myanmar is in the longest civil war in world history. Russia invaded Ukraine with no end to war in sight. Firearms are now the number one leading cause of death for children in the United States.[1] Rates of modern slavery are the highest in human history. War and tragedy surround us on an epic scale.

Similar to today, the nation of Judah watched as world powers decimated countries around them. Ongoing threats of war and destruction echoed throughout Jerusalem, the capital city. An impending sense of fear replaced the perfect peace of the garden. Hope for order and protection seemed far off.

In today's reading, Isaiah gives a futuristic vision of hope. He sees that one day, a restored Jerusalem will be the center of the world. God will reign and dwell with His people on this holy mountain. It will be a center of world peace. Even though the language in this passage might appear specific to a restored Jerusalem, this vision isn't just for this one city—it's also a vision for the entire world.

War will cease. Not only will it end, but it also will be transformed from something completely decimating to something that breeds life. The swords will become plowshares. The spears will become pruning hooks. Instruments formerly used to kill and destroy will be turned into vessels creating life and flourishing. Humankind will restore the tools used for death and destruction into instruments for gardening.

The future of Zion, the holy place where God will dwell, is described here with garden language. In the last days, a world is coming that no longer knows war but has become a fully restored garden. The world will be the dwelling place with God again.

We need to know that a better day is coming. Advent is a fresh reminder that our current pain and suffering don't get to write the end of our story. Heaven and earth will be one again. Peace will replace war. Tragedy will no longer exist. Grief will turn into songs of joy. The tools once meant for destruction will be cultivating beauty and new life.

Hope lives in the waiting for this unseen reality. In the deep wells of disappointment, fear, and tragedy, we hope for a future different from our present. Hope generates our expectations of what's coming to us in the future.[2] In the darkest hours, when pain and suffering seem like they've overtaken us, Jesus offers us fresh hope in what's yet to come. We have this hope to cling to, even when we can't feel anything other than pain. And when we want immediate relief, hope is a willingness to wait in the reality we're living in because we know what's coming.

Jesus walked through the darkness. He experienced the sword and the spears. He intimately knows what it's like to suffer. His very life gives us hope. Yet that hope doesn't necessarily change our current circumstances. If we're going to be a people filled with hope, then we also need to be people who can wait. Isaiah doesn't just leave with ambiguous instructions for waiting. God gives Isaiah words of comfort and hope to relay to His people. God doesn't write off their fear and suffering. Instead, He invites them to walk with the Lord once again.

...come, let us walk in the light of the Lord.
ISAIAH 2:5

The kingdom light is breaking through. It is a present invitation: walk in the light. We can be renewed with hope as we wait for Jesus to return. He gives us hope when we walk in His ways and fix our eyes on Him. It might not change our circumstances or present realities, but being with Jesus reminds us of the ultimate sacrifice He gave us. Jesus paid the price to make this future restored kingdom possible for us.

Again Jesus spoke to them, saying, "I am the light of the world. Whoever follows me will not walk in darkness, but will have the light of life."
JOHN 8:12

This is an open invitation for us today. Hold on to hope. The light of the world has come, and He will come again. He has begun making all things new. Even when hope seems lost, and darkness surrounds us, Jesus has made a way. He is the light of the world. His light will never stop shining. Even if our loss and circumstances can't be changed, when we walk with Jesus, we wait with hope because the light has come and will come again to make all things new.

REFLECTIONS

What does this reveal to us about God?

What verse or words stand out to you in a fresh way?

How does this make you long for the second advent?

"And though a tenth remain in it, it will be burned again, like a terebinth or an oak, whose stump remains when it is felled." The holy seed is its stump.

ISAIAH 6:13

The Holy Seed

Read: Isaiah 6:1–13

An era had ended as the period of peace and prosperity under King Uzziah came to a staggering halt. Yet while the earthly king lay dying, the heavenly king was reigning on high. God looked down on His people from the heavenly throne room, vividly aware of their rebellion towards Him again.

As Isaiah's only recorded vision of heaven, this passage gives us a glimpse into one of the most glorious images of God's throne room in the Old Testament. Seraphim attended to God on His throne. These living flames of pure praise hovered over God in continuous recognition. They covered their faces, acknowledging the overwhelming brightness of God's glory. The seraphim cried out, one after another, worshiping the Lord.

> "Holy, holy, holy is the LORD of hosts;
> The whole earth is full of his glory!"
> **ISAIAH 6:3**

The holiness was overwhelming. Isaiah cried out for mercy shouting "Woe is me!" (Isaiah 6:5) He was overcome not only with his own sin, but also with the sins of God's chosen people. Isaiah recognized he was an imperfect man. The holiness and glory of God's presence filled him with great fear. Culturally, Isaiah knew that appearing improperly before a king could mean death. He was unprepared, undone by his humanness in the light of such holiness.

Despite his imperfection, God used the seraphim to touch Isaiah's lips with a burning coal as an atonement for his sin. Isaiah was cleansed and anointed for commission in the very place God would work through him. Immediately, Isaiah knew forgiveness. When God asked, *"Who shall I send, and who will go for us?"* (Isaiah 6:8), Isaiah didn't hesitate before responding. Because he had just experienced such incredible forgiveness, Isaiah must have felt joyfully compelled to respond.

What's interesting about this passage is that even though Isaiah was merely human, God still chose to use him and speak through him. In his vision, Isaiah was overwhelmed by his imperfection, unable to clean himself up or bring anything of merit to God. He knew he had nothing to give. But God moved towards Isaiah, purifying him with a burning coal to symbolize the offering for his sins. Even when Isaiah had nothing to offer, God still moved towards him.

God listened while Isaiah cried out in submission and acknowledgment of his sin. How wild that God allowed a human to speak in the heavenly throne room—and He listened to Isaiah's response! God hears Isaiah and He personally commissions him to take His messages to the people.

Even though the story in this passage centers on Isaiah's call to become a prophet, there is also a subtle promise for all of God's people within this text. At the end of the message, God tells Isaiah:

> ...The holy seed is its stump.
> **ISAIAH 6:13**

While the city would lie in ruin, a holy seed would survive. God would preserve a remnant. He has never given up on His people despite their continual rebellion. The Israelites in the city of Jerusalem would eventually fall to foreign oppression. Their massive family tree would fall. But God would build something new out of the fallen, upended tree. The stump would bear new roots. God promised a future holy seed—a Messiah to save the people from their sins.

Over and over again, we see God keep His word. He sent His son, Jesus Christ, to fulfill His promise for the future offspring (seed). He continues to unveil a story of redemption for His followers. Despite the consequences and destruction that was coming, God ended His initial words for Isaiah with an invitation to hope.

The holy seed was born in a manger. The people called Him Immanuel, meaning God with us. Jesus was the holy seed. He would fall, knocked down by worldly men, but God's plans were bigger. Jesus would overcome death and establish His kingdom on earth. His life and ministry would plant new seeds with eternal impact.

God is still on the throne, reigning high and receiving continuous praise. He invites us to bring our prayers and our longings before Him. When our present reality feels far removed from the heavenly throne room, we can hold onto this reminder. God's final word is not destruction. It's not pain and it's not tragedy. God's final word is a seed of hope. Jesus, our Messiah, has come to rescue us and give us everlasting life with Him. Our new life begins with Him, our living hope.

Truly, truly, I say to you, whoever hears my word and believes him who sent me has eternal life. He does not come into judgment, but has passed from death to life.
JOHN 5:24

REFLECTIONS

What does this reveal to us about God?

What verse or words stand out to you in a fresh way?

How does this make you long for the second advent?

For to us a child is
born, to us a son
is given; and the
government shall be
upon his shoulder,
and his name
shall be called
Wonderful Counselor,
Mighty God,
Everlasting Father,
Prince of Peace.

ISAIAH 9:6

A Child is Born

Read: Isaiah 9:1–7

Isaiah was assigned a daunting task as God called him to proclaim Judah's impending fall because of their rebellion. God summoned Isaiah not to save the people but to declare their coming demise. The Assyrians would come to overtake Judah. Desolation and thick darkness would cover the land.

When the city would seem to be snuffed out, light would appear in the darkness. The people would rejoice, and oppression would end because the battle was over. A new king was coming. He was coming to bring peace and reign forever because the Lord had not forgotten His promise to His people.

The original audience would have heard this message and hoped that an earthly king was coming. The threat of war was never-ending. World peace was certainly unimaginable in a world where battles were unending. The people wanted a peaceful king. They wanted safety and security.

Our perspective thousands of years later shows that their hope for an earthly king was undoubtedly short-sighted. They wanted an immediate end to their suffering. They wanted a rescuer but didn't necessarily want to live in His kingdom. They had lost their vision of God's kingdom of justice, righteousness, love, and peace while creating their own idols to worship.

This beautiful prophecy of the coming Messiah is one of the most quoted verses at Christmas. During Advent, we consciously acknowledge the waiting for Christ to return. Much like the promise to bring a savior through David's line, God also promises that Jesus will return to bring His kingdom to earth fully. We see glimpses of this promise today in communities where the Holy Spirit is clearly at work. Jesus has been and continues to bring His kingdom light to earth.

God is at work in the most minute details. In verse 1, Isaiah references the land of Zebulun and Naphtali in their coming demise. This specific reference forecasts the initial fall of the Israelites to the Assyrians under King Ahaz. In the same verse, Isaiah also states this place would see Christ's *"glorious way"* for the first time. The same land that would fall to the Assyrians on the darkest day would be the exact spot where Jesus Christ would launch his ministry.

And leaving Nazareth [Jesus] went and lived in Capernaum by the sea, in the territory of Zebulun and Naphtali, so that what was spoken by the prophet Isaiah might be fulfilled: ...From that time Jesus began to preach, saying, "Repent, for the kingdom of heaven is at hand."
MATTHEW 4:13–14, 17

Even though an enemy army overtook Zebulun and Naphtali, God redeems the same land to fulfill His purpose and prophecy. Amid complete desolation and spiritual darkness, the promise of this coming light gives us hope. God will redeem our overwhelming obstacles, suffering, and brokenness. In His kingdom, there will be no grief or pain. Justice and righteousness will reign, bringing joy and peace into unimaginable places.

Peace will reign forevermore. The Prince of Peace will establish a kingdom of peace. Conflict will cease, and shalom will be restored throughout the world. Internal peace will fill God's people, and external peace will be permanent between nations and individuals. This peace gives us freedom and security as citizens in this eternal kingdom. We will dwell forever in a place of perfect peace.

Jesus sits at the right hand of God, awaiting His return. John 14:3 promises us His return. *And if I go and prepare a place for you, I will come again and will take you to myself, that where I am you may be also.* Jesus is preparing a place for us in His kingdom. He isn't sitting idly by in heaven. He is actively at work through the Holy Spirit, bringing His kingdom presence into our lives right now. Jesus gives us wisdom as the Wonderful Counselor. He protects us as Mighty God. He is divine and eternal, an Everlasting Father to lovingly guide us. Jesus brings heavenly peace to the earth as the Prince of Peace.

Jesus has come, and He will come again. Just like God's chosen people who walked in desolation saw the great light, we can hold on to this promise that the light reigns. A light rested above the manger in the dark night sky, shining for all to see. A child was born who would change the world. His kingdom will have no end. Light and peace will reign forevermore.

REFLECTIONS

What does this reveal to us about God?

What verse or words stand out to you in a fresh way?

How does this make you long for the second advent?

There shall come
forth a shoot from the
stump of Jesse, and
a branch from his
roots shall bear fruit.

ISAIAH 11:1

A Peaceful Ruler

Read: Isaiah 11:1–10

Jerusalem's destruction was imminent. God spoke through Isaiah to the people, announcing the upcoming judgment and desolation. The world as they knew it was about to come crashing down. Despite Isaiah's warnings, the people chose not to repent and turn back to God. The people had hardened their hearts. Although they knew God and experienced His faithfulness and protection, they had gotten distracted creating their own sanctuaries.

In many ways, we experience similar distractions today. We tend to fill our lives with so much stuff. There are always better vacations, activities to participate in, new things to purchase, or the next workout plan. We might have seen God move in incredible ways in the past, but we tend to forget quickly. As life goes on, we can lose sight of answered prayers and met desires. Instead, our eyes focus on the things surrounding us that give us a false sense of comfort and peace.

The Israelites were lost, unaware they were even in rebellion. Though they heard Isaiah's warning for their future judgment, the people paradoxically moved further away from God. With their hearts undeterred, God would let their enemies overtake their land, their houses, and their families. What had been a vibrant city would be utterly destroyed and left in ruins.

Despite the near-total destruction, God would not forget His people. His promise lay in the symbol of the stump among the burnt ashes. Though their sin grieved Him, God would not wipe out the Israelites. He guaranteed a future Messiah was coming. From the stump, a budding shoot would grow into a new branch to continue God's story of redemption and restoration. The tree fell, but God's story wasn't over. The promised ruler was still coming.

New leadership would arise from David's line. The Spirit of the Lord would rest on Him and guide His steps. He would delight in the Lord and rule with justice and righteousness over the people. The world would exist in perfect harmony under His reign. He would restore the garden to its former glory. Animals would coexist peacefully with children. The whole earth would be full of God's presence and knowledge.

The stump would grow fresh roots. A new shoot would grow out of the deep roots. The king would still come from David's line of descendants. Jesus was the root—He was the promised offspring and Messiah.

"I, Jesus, have sent my angel to testify to you
about these things for the churches. I am the root and the
descendant of David, the bright morning star."
REVELATION 22:16

Jesus came to rescue and restore God's people in an everlasting deliverance. He came to rule as the Prince of Peace. In this almost utopian vision of the new heavens and new earth, Isaiah invites us back to remember the garden, where animals existed in perfect harmony with man. God will restore the relationships between animals, man, and all creatures to the state of Eden. The weak will no longer be the prey of the strong. All of creation will dwell in perfect peace under His care.

One day, we, too, will exist in perfect harmony with Jesus as our King. In the Advent season, we await the promise of Jesus's return to reign. While we wait, we trust Jesus to rule over our hearts. Our circumstances can cause us to look around and see all kinds of distractions and suffering. Our families have broken relationships, children rebel, poverty overwhelms our nation, and crime stirs fear within us. From when we wake up in the morning to when we sleep at night, we are constantly deciding where to fix our attention and focus.

Isaiah tells us how Jesus would handle the waiting amidst the hard. It was written about Him before He ever even came to earth.

> And his delight shall be in the fear of the Lord.
> **ISAIAH 11:3**

Only in Jesus's kingdom is there peace. We can find His delight–no matter our circumstances–by walking in God's ways and submitting ourselves to His plan. Just like Israel remembered God's faithfulness to them, we can also remember God's faithfulness to us. We start with our own stories. When we were lost, He first found us.

Jesus is not just the ruler of the nations, but He's also the ruler of our hearts. The good news of His kingdom is available for all if we repent and believe. Jesus lived the perfect life and sacrificed Himself on our behalf so we could dwell with our sinless God. He is our Peaceful Ruler despite our distractible hearts. He is our Messiah—the Savior we never deserved.

REFLECTIONS

What does this reveal to us about God?

What verse or words stand out to you in a fresh way?

How does this make you long for the second advent?

"Behold, God is my salvation; I will trust, and will not be afraid; for the Lord God is my strength and my song, and he has become my salvation."

ISAIAH 12:2

DAY 05

We Remember

Read: Isaiah 12:1–6

Isaiah's words do not only carry warning, but they also cast hope. God's story for His people is always one of hope. Judgment day is coming, but for those faithful to God, this is a day to long for with joy and excitement. God will return to dwell with His people. He will bring restoration to the whole earth. God will replace pain and suffering with joy and praise.

It's hard to imagine what our lives will look like when we're with Jesus. We get glimpses of heaven and the restored earth in the Gospels and the book of Revelation. But there is still so much mystery. How can we long for a place we do not yet know or understand?

> For we know that the whole creation has been groaning together in the pains of childbirth until now. And not only the creation, but we ourselves, who have the firstfruits of the Spirit, groan inwardly as we wait eagerly for adoption as sons, the redemption of our bodies. For in this hope we were saved. Now hope that is seen is not hope.
> For who hopes for what he sees?
> **ROMANS 8:22–24**

All creation groans with longing to be made new. We all desire a cure for cancer and sickness. We wish we didn't have to say goodbye to people we love. We watch the news and don't understand why people hurt others.

We watch natural disasters spin out of control and quietly whisper prayers for people we've never met. Christian or not, we all long to see restored people, places, and things.

Isaiah's words carry a promise and a comfort that is still for God's people today. The day is coming when we will give thanks. The brokenness of this world will pass away. God will return to dwell with us once again. We will give thanks and proclaim God's name and deeds to the ends of the earth. The world will celebrate, singing songs of celebration and praise.

In the meantime, during Advent, as we await this day, we recount God's faithfulness by remembering what He has done. The people of Israel remembered God's faithfulness with their escape from slavery in Egypt. They heard stories from their ancestors of God's provision for them in the wilderness. They had lived in and experienced the Promised Land. They knew God was faithful because they had seen and experienced it. We, too, can see and remember God's faithfulness in the waiting.

Whether you've been walking with Jesus for a week or a lifetime, we see God's faithfulness in His willingness to rescue us from ourselves. He invites us to join the kingdom family when we place our hope in Him. We celebrate that Jesus was willing to die for our sins so that we could live in His eternal kingdom, worshiping our Savior. We remember God's faithfulness to us through His offer for everlasting life. We celebrate that God has saved us and is still at work within us through the power of the Holy Spirit.

Today, we give thanks to God for our salvation. We hope for things we might not fully see or understand but trust to be true because we have experienced God's faithfulness to come after our hearts. Like the Israelites longing for a new king, we long for Jesus to return. We remember what He's done because we've seen God's faithfulness in sending His son to dwell on earth. We recount the birth of Jesus when God fulfilled His promise to bring a savior through David's line. We hold onto this promise while waiting, placing our hope in the one who was, is, and is to come.

"I am the Alpha and the Omega," says the Lord God, "who is and who was and who is to come, the Almighty."

REVELATION 1:8

REFLECTIONS

What does this reveal to us about God?

What verse or words stand out to you in a fresh way?

How does this make you long for the second advent?

"Then a throne will be
established in steadfast
love, and on it will
sit in faithfulness in
the tent of David one
who judges and seeks
justice and is swift to
do righteousness."

ISAIAH 16:5

Hope for Justice

Read: Isaiah 16:1–7

Much like genealogies, Isaiah chapters 13–24 are tempting to breeze over, lumping this section into one repeating judgment for the nations. Reading about God's judgment isn't easy. Remembering God's anger and wrath is a sobering reminder that there are consequences for those who reject God's authority. Each of these nations shared one thing in common: their pride had led them into deep-seated arrogance and rejection of the one true God.

Even though these chapters can be difficult to process, they have a critical message for us today. One day, people over all of the earth will recognize Yahweh's sovereignty and will be held accountable for their actions. Our God is a just God. He has the final authority to punish the wicked. The Day of the Lord will come when God will judge all people. Everyone will experience this final judgment.

Through a series of poems, Isaiah announces the coming destruction and downfall of the nations because of their rampant pride and injustice. Isaiah saw another empire arising after Assyria, who would also attack Jerusalem and succeed in destroying it. Assyria's world power would fall to Babylon, a nation even more prideful and arrogant than Assyria. Babylon's kings claimed they were higher than other gods (Isaiah 14:13–14). Within these chapters, Isaiah verbally confronts Babylon and Israel's neighbors, who also live with the same pride and injustice. Each nation would come to ruin for their arrogance and rejection of God.

Specifically, in our passage today, Isaiah prophesies about the future downfall of Moab. Their neighboring countries were well aware of the Moabites blatant pride. Moab had family ties with Israel, but did not share Israel's faith. Moab is referenced several times within the Old Testament as an evil influence and enemy known for their pride. We know from other Scripture that the Moabites dwelled in the rocky hillside. The image in verse 2 of birds fleeing like a scattered nest gives us a picture of God upending their home, sending them out. The nation of Moab would fall, and the people would disperse into neighboring countries. The refugees, likely women and children, were weak and defenseless.

Later in Isaiah, we'll see Yahweh lament over the people of Moab. However, in the passage we read today, God hears their plea for help but chooses to defer action to the coming Messiah. Instead of rescuing them from their oppressor, God points the people to a new king coming to bring justice and peace to the world. The future king would establish justice and righteousness in the world through David's line.

Although it's challenging to think about future judgment, our hearts also long for justice. Injustice overwhelms our cities. Human trafficking is the third-largest crime industry in the world. Global Estimates for Modern Slavery tell us that nearly 50 million people live in modern slavery today.[3] 64% of Americans are living paycheck to paycheck.[4] Poverty is rampant across the globe and right down the street. Mental health crises have never been higher. We can hardly keep up with all the latest sad stories on our newsfeed. We work hard to protect ourselves and our loved ones, but we can't seem to keep evil at bay.

While participating in social justice efforts now can be the fruit of our faith, we await a day when righteousness will reign, and justice will be served. The Day of the Lord is coming. The Judge will come to rule the world and cast a verdict on those who walk in pride and reject God's sovereign authority. Oppressors will face their final fate. God will punish the arrogant and unrepentant. But for those who believe in Jesus and acknowledge Him as our Lord and Savior, this day should bring great comfort. It reassures us that evil will not have the final say. Jesus has come to overcome the darkness.

The light shines in the darkness, and the darkness has not overcome it.
JOHN 1:5

We can hope for perfect justice because we know Jesus is returning to bring an end to all oppression. He's coming to build a kingdom of justice and righteousness. Jesus will bring freedom to the persecuted. He'll restore those who've been rejected and abandoned. The darkness will not overcome the light. Jesus is our hope for justice.

REFLECTIONS

What does this reveal to us about God?

What verse or words stand out to you in a fresh way?

How does this make you long for the second advent?

He will swallow up
death forever; and
the LORD God will
wipe away tears from
all faces, and the
reproach of his people
he will take away
from all the earth,
for the LORD
has spoken.

ISAIAH 25:8

The Banquet Feast

Read: Isaiah 25:6–10

Gathering around the table for the holidays can always be a bit nostalgic. At Christmas time, we unpack the same ornaments and put up decorations passed down to us by our parents and grandparents. We practice traditions and participate in festive activities with family and friends. As life happens, some Christmases are more joyful than others. There have been years when we gathered around the table and felt the longing pain of someone we love who was missing from the celebration. Like an old friend, grief knows when to come knocking and remind us that a person we love is missing from our celebration.

Isaiah 25–27 concludes the previous chapters on the coming judgment and downfall of the nations. While it might seem fitting, this section doesn't end in grief and desolation. Instead, it ends with a comparison of the coming new Jerusalem, where God will return to dwell with His people. In chapter 25, a song breaks out unannounced, inviting us into a scene of God's new reign, specifically a banquet feast. With the best wines and richest foods, the Lord asks His people to share in His joyful abundance on the restored mountain of Zion, where He will dwell.

Let's use our imaginations for a moment to picture this banquet. All of God's people will come together to celebrate and worship. Envision the people you love who are no longer with us: the children lost too soon, the grandparents who have gone ahead, the legacies you've never met, and the one you wish was still at your Christmas table. Picture the kingdom celebration banquet. The joy will be unparalleled. The magnificence is too much to comprehend.

The celebration will be so joyous that it's nearly impossible for us to imagine, but that doesn't diminish the pain and difficulty of our waiting today. We can see the light at the end of the tunnel, but we're not there yet. In the meantime, while we wait amidst hard days, we must keep reminding ourselves what and who we are waiting for.

> It will be said on that day, "Behold, this is our God;
> we have waited for him, that he might save us.
> This is the Lord; we have waited for him;
> let us be glad and rejoice in his salvation."
> **ISAIAH 25:9**

Isaiah prophesied a future time after the final judgment where God would save His people. He would swallow up death forever. God would send His beloved son to rescue His people.

Yeshua is a short form of the Hebrew name *Yehoshua*, which means 'Yahweh saves.' *Yeshua* is the personal name of Jesus. His very name means savior. God's people didn't have to wait until the final judgment. God was gracious enough to send His son, *Yeshua*, to save us.

As we pause to reflect on this Advent season, *Yeshua's* arrival is the most important milestone to celebrate. The bold claim that Isaiah and other prophets made thousands of years ago about a coming Savior has come true. God has been faithful to His promises.

John 4:42 states it best *"...It is no longer because of what you said that we believe, for we have heard for ourselves, and we know that this is indeed the Savior of the world."*

Today, we also await *Yeshua*, the one who would come to rescue us, redeem us, and restore our world. He is coming again to bring an end to suffering. Death will be no more. There will be no more tears or grief, no more goodbyes or not yet. Jesus will turn our sorrow into joy. He will tear the veil, and we will finally have clear eyes to see and experience glory.

This day is what we are waiting for. We long for the moment we arrive at the banquet feast where we will dine and celebrate with our Savior, King Jesus. He will swallow up death and suffering forever. In the meantime, while we wait in our broken world and break bread with those we love, we hold onto this promised future banquet celebration to come.

REFLECTIONS

What does this reveal to us about God?

What verse or words stand out to you in a fresh way?

How does this make you long for the second advent?

"You keep him in perfect peace whose mind is stayed on you, because he trusts in you. Trust in the LORD forever, for the LORD God is an everlasting rock."

ISAIAH 26:3-4

Rock of Ages

Read: Isaiah 26:1-9

Isaiah 26 continues with the picture describing the restored city of Jerusalem. A new song of salvation breaks out as Isaiah proclaims the final victory celebration. *In that day,* (Isaiah 26:1), the city will be rebuilt, fortified, and ready to receive guests who kept the faith. The gates will open to welcome the righteous. Peace will dwell within the people who have trusted the Lord. Those in need will experience the protection they have longed for.

What's interesting about this celebratory song of salvation is that it does not focus on what the people would be saved from. The song doesn't exalt their deliverance. Instead, it focuses on the Lord Himself. Isaiah wasn't only urging everyone to put their faith in God, repent, and believe in the hope of being rescued from their current circumstances. He was casting a vision for people to look to God as their everlasting rock, trusting Him as a way of life.

Simply put, God wants to rescue us so we can dwell with Him. We need to be saved from ourselves to be with Him. The heart of a true believer is not just to end up in heaven to avoid hell. The ultimate goal is to live with and worship Immanuel, *God with us.*

Jesus came to dwell as the fulfillment of God's promise to save His people and live among them. He is the true Prince of Peace. To experience this peace, we have to trust the Lord. From that place of trust, He can bring us peace. More than a happy or tranquil feeling, peace is an invitation to rest in the finished work of what Jesus has accomplished on our behalf. It transcends our circumstances.

As we fix our eyes on Jesus, we experience God's peace and presence today through the power of the Holy Spirit. He is at work within us to give us an abundance of supernatural peace when we look to Him for protection. He is the rock on which we rest.

We long to dwell with God because His presence is a sweet place of refuge and protection. When life is in chaos and everything surrounding us feels like a terrible storm, God is our rock and safe harbor. When we aren't sure if we will make it, God gives us firm footing. When the storm seems like it will consume us, God gives us a safe place of protection on his solid ground. Augustus M. Toplady drew the inspiration for his famous hymn, *Rock of Ages*, from these same verses.

> Rock of Ages, cleft for me,
> Let me hide myself in Thee.

God's presence is the safe harbor, firm on the rock, amidst the storms of life. He alone can provide the safety we long for. Scripture continuously illustrates the metaphor of God as the rock.

> The Lord is my rock and my fortress and my deliverer, my God,
> my rock, in whom I take refuge, my shield, and the horn of my
> salvation, my stronghold.
> **PSALM 18:2**

The Lord is the unchanging rock. He is our foundation. God is unmoving. He is firm. He holds us up. We can trust His solid rock foundation. When we fix our eyes on Him, He will give us His peace. Focusing on Him shifts our gaze from ourselves to our God. Through the mysterious power of the Holy Spirit, we can experience deep peace that surpasses our understanding.

As we wait in this Advent season when things seem unstable around us, we can take comfort in this word: Fix your eyes on Jesus. Trust in His unfolding plan. Set your feet upon the rock. He is a safe place to land.

REFLECTIONS

What does this reveal to us about God?

What verse or words stand out to you in a fresh way?

How does this make you long for the second advent?

Therefore thus
says the Lord GOD,
"Behold, I am the one
who has laid as a
foundation in Zion, a
stone, a tested stone, a
precious cornerstone,
of a sure foundation:
'Whoever believes
will not be in haste.'"

ISAIAH 28:16

A Firm Foundation

Read: Isaiah 28:14–16

We typically can't see our foundations. They live hidden away, tucked under flooring, subfloor, and concrete layers. Even though they might not be visible outside, the foundation holds a structure together. The builder builds this section first. This support is critical for the safety and durability of the building. A foundation establishes the necessary base on solid ground.

Jerusalem had lost its firm foundation. The leaders had lost faith in God to protect them from neighboring countries. In an act of reckless confidence, the country's leaders had begun making treaties with other nations like Egypt to try and defend themselves against the Assyrians. Isaiah warned the leaders that only repenting and trusting in God could protect them. Isaiah went as far as to compare their treaty with a covenant of death because they had placed their trust in making allies for protection instead of God.

The Israelites would likely not have recognized this promise of a Messiah in Isaiah's prophecy. They would have been considering this promise in light of a physical temple. They couldn't see what God was already working to accomplish. Despite the people's response and continued unwillingness to repent, God offered mercy and grace because of His deep love and compassion for His children.

Isaiah's words in chapter 28 cast judgment on Jerusalem for their lack of faith, but they also point to the work that God was already doing. He was clearing the people, places, and things that weren't bringing Him honor to rebuild a new foundation.

A cornerstone in ancient times was the largest and most established stone in a building's foundation. The builder would center the rest of the building around this specific stone. In verse 16, God promises a cornerstone would come. It would be laid as the foundation and tested for its strength. Jesus was the cornerstone. He would be tested and tried. He would be steadfast and unmoving. He would be the faithful rock and foundation. God would use His life and ministry to build the Church.

The promised cornerstone here is so significant. No longer would God dwell in a physical temple. Through the Holy Spirit, God would return to live **with** His people and **within** His people. He would replace the temple in Jerusalem with a temple inside the hearts of those who have put their faith and trust in Him.

Built on the foundation of the apostles and prophets, Christ Jesus himself being the cornerstone, in whom the whole structure, being joined together, grows into a holy temple in the Lord. In him you also are being built together into a dwelling place for God by the Spirit.

EPHESIANS 2:20–22

Jesus would be rejected by men but chosen by God to establish the foundations of the Church for God's people. We will be granted eternal citizenship through Jesus's life, death, and resurrection as part of God's family. He would no longer be separate from His people. The Holy Spirit would come to take residency within those faithful followers of Yahweh.

For thousands of years, believers have built on the foundation of the prophets and apostles. With Christ as our cornerstone, we have a solid foundation. We can place our hope in the rock that carries our burdens and protects us from the storm. He holds all things together. Jesus is our shelter from the storm. He is rest for the weary, the hope for the hopeless, and our steadfast rock and Redeemer.

Even though we might not always be able to see Jesus, we can trust He is still there. Under all the layers, the foundation remains steady. When our anxiety increases and conflicts rise, we don't have to look around for security. We don't have to keep running to find other things to protect us. Trust is how we get to experience God. When we put our hope and faith in Jesus, we can experience new heights of peace in the stability that a foundation gives us. Nothing else can satisfy and get us solid ground apart from Jesus.

Slow down this Advent season and experience Jesus's sturdy foundation. He is safe, steady, and secure. The good news begins in unseen places. On His rock is the safest place to be.

We can hold to this promise from the final lyrics of *How Firm a Foundation*:

The soul that on Jesus has leaned for repose
I will not, I will not desert to his foes
That soul, though all hell should endeavor to shake
I'll never, no never, no never forsake

REFLECTIONS

What does this reveal to us about God?

What verse or words stand out to you in a fresh way?

How does this make you long for the second advent?

And the effect of
righteousness will be
peace, and the result
of righteousness,
quietness and trust
forever. My people
will abide in a peaceful
habitation, in secure
dwellings, and in quiet
resting places.

ISAIAH 32:17-18

A Presence of Peace

Read: Isaiah 32:9–20

In chapter 32, Isaiah gives a specific warning to the complacent women of Judah. Their time is short, and the women need to be placing their priorities in the right things. The coming harvest was about to fail, and the people would desert the city. The drought would cause dryness to fall across the land, ending their affluent lifestyle. Everything they had put their hope and worth into would soon crumble around them.

A similar warning still holds for us today. The things outside of Jesus we've put our trust in to satisfy us can't hold. According to a study by The Pew Research Group in 2022, Christianity is rapidly declining in the United States. If the rate of deconversion continues to accelerate, as it has since the 1990s, those who would classify themselves as Christians will drop to under 35% of the American population by 2070.[5] The church in America is sleepy. Even though the Gospel is still at work, many people have become indifferent to their faith.

In the United States, we can work hard, get a decent job, and have somewhere to call home. It's not quite the American dream, but a picture of what our culture tells us will give us joy. Go to school, attend college, graduate, get a job, work hard, earn money, get married, buy a house, have kids, get a better job, and so on. Every season gives us new goals and things to long for out of our reach. It's easy to believe we'll finally find rest and genuine happiness when we reach that next stage.

Wealth has made us complacent. Marketing tells us that the things we buy will make us a little happier. We can get so caught up in consumerism that we can act like we don't *need* Jesus. Or if we do need Him, it's just on Sundays and not in the ongoing rhythms of our daily lives. We can miss out on caring for those around us because we're too stuck in our worlds, attending to our desires.

Isaiah called these Israelite women back to focus their affections on their Provider. They were about to enter a difficult season, but Isaiah prophesied that it would only last *until the Spirit is poured upon us from on high.* (Isaiah 32:15) This futuristic picture of the Spirit is explicitly referring to Jesus. He would be the living water, coming to end their physical drought. He would be their Deliverer from the dead fruit and deserted city. While the people would have heard this promise and longed for a new earthly king to save them, God promised something even more remarkable.

God would pour out His Spirit upon His people. The active presence of His Spirit will bring justice and righteousness to the land. From this same Spirit, a king would come to reign to initiate righteousness, quietness, and trust. The effect will be peace. We can have quiet, peaceful places to dwell because of Jesus.

In the midst of the people forgetting to worship and honor God, He was still faithful to His promise to bring a savior to the world. Similarly, today, even though our complacent hearts have turned to worldly things, God gives us a similar commitment. Things in this world will be hard; they might be desolate, dark, and lonely. But that isn't the end of our story.

A king is coming to reign on high. He will bring righteousness and peace. He will restore the dry land to living water. The Holy Spirit will pour out on the people, and we will gather and worship him. We will no longer be distracted by everything we could buy for momentary satisfaction. Instead, our hearts and mouths will overflow, singing praises for our beloved Savior.

REFLECTIONS

What does this reveal to us about God?

What verse or words stand out to you in a fresh way?

How does this make you long for the second advent?

Say to those who have
an anxious heart,
"Be strong; fear not!
Behold, your God will
come with vengeance,
with the recompense
of God. He will come
and save you."

ISAIAH 35:4

Desolation to Deliverance

Read: Isaiah 35:1–10

We've reached the climax of the story. The continuous threat of judgment and destruction has finally reached its breaking point. In Isaiah 34, we read that judgment has finally fallen on the nations. The words paint a vivid picture of The Day of Judgment, and it isn't easy to read. Isaiah 34:9 tells us that water goes dry, soil breaks down into chemicals, and the land transforms into a burning field. The smoke never ends. The world is a bloody, chaotic mess. It's tempting to skip over because it can be overwhelming.

In the prior chapter, Isaiah 34 tells a story similar to the final scene in Harry Potter. Rumors have been swirling for years about Lord Voldemort and his enemy army. Everyone is scared of his powers. He exudes darkness and brings death to whoever is in his path. The plot twists and turns until the final confrontation arrives. Harry and his friends are ready to fight and sacrifice it all to save humankind. In the final battle, Harry confronts Lord Voldemort face to face. The altercation inevitably escalates. But when it seems like the good will conquer it all, Lord Voldemort strikes Harry down. For a moment, evil seems to win. All hope feels lost.

Verses from Chapter 34 paint a similar desolate scene. Darkness and destruction seem to overtake the world. For a moment, it appears that evil has won. The world waits with anticipation for the final verdict.

Scholars tell us that this Day of the Lord in Isaiah 34 is a metaphorical and literal prophecy. Judah would fall. The Israelites would become exiles in Babylon. But more than that, God is giving us a picture of the final judgment to come at the end of time. While the desolation to come is more than our wildest imaginations can handle, God doesn't leave us in anticipation, wondering if evil will have the final say.

Immediately following the description of the final judgment, God proceeds with a promise for His followers in Chapter 35, which we read today. The wilderness will flourish once again. The glory of the Lord will fill the existence and create a new order and life. God's presence will bring overwhelming glory to the world. Light will supersede the darkness. Supernatural restoration will bring sight to the blind and heal the bodies of the sick. Water will produce a source of life to end thirst. The world will flourish in this perfect, restored new kingdom.

Jesus faced this same destruction. After Jesus died on the cross, He descended into hell. Jesus experienced the worst of death on our behalf. He rose again and ascended to be with the Father until His final return. On Easter weekend, we tend to recognize Good Friday, when Jesus died, and celebrate Easter morning on Sunday. But what about the quiet Saturday between Friday night and Sunday morning? What happened when all hope felt lost? Jesus's disciples waited in that same tense anticipation. Their fearless leader had died. Their beloved friend was supposed to save the world.

The gospel is good news because Jesus overcame death. Jesus came to the world to be our Savior. He has promised us that there is so much more for those who put their hope and trust in Him. Much like the disciples' fear in the final moments after Jesus's death, we too, hold our breath in anticipation. We want assurance that the good guy wins. Collectively, we sit on the edge of our seats at the story's climax and ask, ***will goodness or evil prevail?***

Verse 4 in today's reading is God's words through Isaiah, *"Be strong; fear not!"* We no longer have to let fear rule over our future. Jesus will return once again with one purpose, "He will come and save you." (Isaiah 35:4)

Jesus is coming back. As we sit in this Advent season and await the Day of Final Judgment, God's Word speaks to us. *Fear not. Be strong.* He is coming to return for His bride to restore this world with the fullness of His glory. The deaf will hear. The blind will see. Light and life will fill the world forever. Good will overcome evil in the very end.

REFLECTIONS

What does this reveal to us about God?

What verse or words stand out to you in a fresh way?

How does this make you long for the second advent?

"For I will defend this city to save it, for my own sake and for the sake of my servant David."

ISAIAH 37:35

The King Who Reigns

Read: Isaiah 37:33–35

While most of the book of Isaiah is poetic, chapters 36-39 interject with a historical narrative that positions the book for the next series of prophecies. In these narrative chapters, King Hezekiah sits on the throne in Judah with Isaiah to guide him as God's messenger.

During Hezekiah's reign, the whole area of West Palestine became submissive to Assyria. As Isaiah had prophesied, the Assyrians conquered and overcame prominent nations. Judah felt the tension of war, assaulted by Assyria and hard-pressed by other countries for ongoing alliances.

God supernaturally rescued Jerusalem from the impending onslaught of the Assyrian army. God protected Jerusalem by striking an army of 185,000 men outside the city gate. Because of Hezekiah's faith, God delivered Judah from their impending destruction, and Jerusalem survived unharmed.

While God spared the Israelites from the Assyrian army, a new enemy, Babylon, began to grow. Isaiah prophesied the coming Babylonian exile. He declared the Babylonians would one day be the army to carry off God's people from Jerusalem. These chapters set the scene for the next section of he story.

Up to this point, one central theme has been **the king who reigns.** We've read about earthly kings who had hard hearts against God, like King Ahaz, and kings who pursued God's heart but messed up along the way, like Hezekiah. We've looked at the promise of the future king to come. And we've seen the Lord reigning on high, sovereign over all things. Throughout each of the stories, one thing is obvious. God always stood by His promise to bring a future king and restored kingdom.

Over and over again, in the story of Isaiah, we see the Israelite's lack of faith in God and rebellion against Him. Yet, time after time, God still chose to remain faithful to His people and promises. While the next chapter of the Israelite's story will take them out of Jerusalem to Babylon in exile, God would remain committed to preserving His people. He would not destroy them for their sin. God would not forget them in exile. He would remain faithful to continue their story. He was still at work, establishing His kingdom through His people.

Much like God faithfully preserved the Israelites despite their rebellion, He also remains loyal to us. God makes a way for us. Despite our sin and hard-heartedness, He doesn't give up on our hearts. He pursues and restores us back to Him. He reveals Himself to us through the Holy Spirit and the Word.

God has fulfilled His promise to bring a future king. Jesus Christ was born in Bethlehem, just a few miles outside the same city of Jerusalem. He wouldn't come as expected. He wouldn't sit on a formal throne or arrive with a grand proclamation from the sky. Jesus came as an innocent baby boy to set His people free.

REFLECTIONS

What does this reveal to us about God?

What verse or words stand out to you in a fresh way?

How does this make you long for the second advent?

Come, Thou Long Expected Jesus

Come, thou long expected Jesus
Born to set Thy people free;
From our fears and sins release us;
Let us find our rest in Thee
Israel's Strength and Consolation
Hope of all the earth Thou art;
Dear Desire of every nation
Joy of every longing heart

Born Thy people to deliver
Born a child and yet a King
Born to reign in us forever
Now Thy gracious kingdom bring
By Thine own eternal Spirit
Rule in all our hearts alone;
By Thine all sufficient merit
Raise us to Thy glorious throne

A 1744 Advent carol written by Charles Wesley

Go on up to a high
mountain, O Zion,
herald of good news;
lift up your voice
with strength,
O Jerusalem, herald
of good news; lift it
up, fear not; say to
the cities of Judah,
"Behold your God!"

ISAIAH 40:9

The Good News

Read: Isaiah 40:1–11

In today's reading, we wake up, so to speak, in a new era. Isaiah 40 transitions the storyline from Jerusalem at the turn of the seventh century BC to Babylon in the mid-sixth century BC. We've fast-forwarded roughly 150 years into the future. There are no references over the intervening century and a half. Everything was silent. Jerusalem had fallen, and the Babylonians had taken the Israelites into captivity. For years, they had waited for liberation, impatient to return home.

While there remains to be some scholarly discussion about whether Isaiah wrote this futuristic view through God's prophetic enablement, Isaiah's purview of the future exile gives us a clear insight into God's heart for His people. The story continues to ask, ***will God rescue and restore His people?***

The Israelites had been in exile for 70 years. The Babylonians had destroyed their homes and left the city in ruins. For decades, the Israelites had struggled to assimilate into a new culture. They were living in a foreign land, under another government's leadership, separated from what had once been their spiritual and physical home in Jerusalem. They didn't have a temple. God was no longer dwelling among them.

After seventy years of silence in exile, God finally speaks.

Comfort, comfort my people, says your God.

ISAIAH 40:1

God's people needed comfort. They needed to know that God was still there and that He was still for them. The announcement came from the heavenly throne room to the prophet Isaiah. We read here that a voice spoke three times in Isaiah 40 in verses 3, 6, and 9.

God began by declaring for His heavenly attendants to comfort His people. The repetition of the word 'comfort' emphasizes the depth of His emotional response. He hadn't forgotten them. Their prayers hadn't gone unnoticed. He had heard their repentant cries and was ready to forgive their sins.

God's cry for comfort first leads His messengers to His glory. In verse 3, a voice cries: *"In the wilderness prepare the way of the LORD; make straight in the desert a highway for our God."*

God was already preparing the hearts of His people. He would make a way at His coming to remove every obstacle. He would forge a path for His people to see and encounter His glory. *"And the glory of the Lord shall be revealed, and all flesh shall see it together..."* (Isaiah 40:5) Mark begins his Gospel account with this very story.

The beginning of the gospel of Jesus Christ, the Son of God.
As it is written in Isaiah the prophet, "Behold, I send my
messenger before your face, who will prepare your way,
the voice of one crying in the wilderness: Prepare the
way of the Lord, make his paths straight..."

MARK 1:1–3

The beginning of Jesus's story began long before His birth. Isaiah prophesied a future messiah who would bring good news to Jerusalem. His message started with a reminder for the people: *"Behold your God."*

(Isaiah 40:9) Experience His glory. See the way that He is making for you. Look at His faithfulness. Rejoice in His response. Behold Him.

The voice continues with two other messages for the Israelites. *The word of our God will stand forever.* (Isaiah 40:8) God's voice in His Word points us to the glory of God as His character displays it. He's not just given us Himself, He's also given us His living Word.

> And the Word became flesh and dwelt among us...
> **JOHN 1:14**

Jesus himself became the living Word. God prepared the hearts of the people. He made a way for Jesus to enter the world to be the fulfillment of the good news. There is comfort for God's people! He has made a way for Jesus to dwell within our hearts today. Jesus lived the sinless life we could never live so that we could participate firsthand in the return to Zion. He has made a way for us. Shout the good news about Jesus from the mountaintops. *Behold your God!*

REFLECTIONS

What does this reveal to us about God?

What verse or words stand out to you in a fresh way?

How does this make you long for the second advent?

Fear not, for I am
with you; be not
dismayed, for I am
your God; I will
strengthen you,
I will help you,
I will uphold you
with my righteous
right hand.

ISAIAH 41:10

Fear Not

Read: Isaiah 41:8–10

Many cultures and people groups have long considered fear to be a weakness. Verses like Isaiah 41:10 have been designed and printed on thousands of materials for decades. From t-shirts to flowery mugs and cute Pinterest images, "Don't be afraid" and "Fear not" have been used often as clever slogans to push against all kinds of fear.

In Isaiah 41, God spoke to a particular group of people. He was talking to His chosen group—the Israelites. He wanted to bring them home to restore their city. And as He began to speak to them again after a long period of exile, God started with some very intentional, comforting words.

> Fear not, for I am with you.
> **ISAIAH 41:10**

God reminds the Israelites that He is with them. Even though they hadn't heard His voice in a long time, God had never abandoned them. He was still their God. He hadn't left them. They didn't need to fear what was coming because He was still in their midst.

God doesn't just instruct His people not to have feelings of fear. He gives them the reason they don't need to be afraid. Verse 10 continues, *Be not dismayed, for I am your God.* They didn't need to be fearful because God controlled the situation. Dismayed here means "to dart glances this way and that as if not knowing where to look for safety."[6] God reminded them that He was their safety. He was with them. He would make their way on their behalf. They didn't need to be afraid because He would again go before them.

While it's easy to get lost in understanding *why* God would let His beloved people suffer in exile for so long, this verse reminds us that sometimes trying to **understand** keeps us from **seeing** the bigger picture. The more significant issue here is that He was still their God. Despite their sin and disobedience, God hadn't left them. He was still with them and for them. Not only was He still there for them, but He had been there the whole time. God had not abandoned them even when they felt like their prayers had gone unanswered and their tears were unseen.

It can be tough to believe God is at work when we can't see Him or experience His presence. Still, He promises He will give us what we need to remember that He is our God. He tells the Israelites, *I will strengthen you, I will help you.* (Isaiah 41:10) He would equip them with all they need through His strength. He would make a way when it felt like there was no way.

God further promised, *I will uphold you with my righteous right hand.* (Isaiah 41:10) Not only would He strengthen them, but He would also hold them up with His extending embrace. They would stand under His protective reign. God would make their steps steadfast and protect them in their pursuit to glorify Him.

In Scripture, God offers His right hand to uphold His people. Being at the leader's right hand symbolizes authority and power for the person on the right side. God's Word tells us that Jesus sits at the right hand of God today.

> Christ Jesus is the one who died—more than that, who was raised—who is at the right hand of God, who indeed is interceding for us.
>
> **ROMANS 8:34**

Jesus sits at the right hand of God. Through the Holy Spirit's work, Jesus still upholds God's people today. He strengthens us and reminds us that our God is still with us despite our sins. Like the Israelites, we continually come to Him with repentance and belief.

The phrase *"Fear not"* doesn't come with a warning to put away our fears and anxieties. "Fear not" comes with an invitation for us to know that He is our God. The very same God who rescued the Israelites still extends these promises to believers today. He will make a way for us. He will strengthen and help us. He will protect us and keep us walking towards Him.

Much like the Israelites' anticipation after hearing God speak about their deliverance after so many years of silence, the Church today longs to hear about our future salvation. We worship and serve the same God. Your Redeemer is the Holy One of Israel!

Our Redeemer delivers His people. Jesus purchased a guarantee for us to spend eternity with Him. We, too, begin our journey with belief and repentance. We look to Jesus, our Savior, and allow Him to strengthen us and give us all we need to sustain our faith. Fear Not; the best is yet to come with Him.

REFLECTIONS

What does this reveal to us about God?

What verse or words stand out to you in a fresh way?

How does this make you long for the second advent?

Behold my servant,
whom I uphold, my
chosen, in whom my
soul delights; I have
put my Spirit upon
him; he will bring
forth justice to the
nations.

ISAIAH 42:1

The Chosen Servant

Read: Isaiah 42:1–9

Within this chapter, God continues to reveal more about His coming Messiah. The promised Savior would come as a *"servant."* This striking descriptor reveals the unique nature of the promised King. Everything about this King was unexpected. The Israelites surely would have assumed God would send an earthly king with pomp and status. Yet a servant couldn't possibly equate with a king. God had bigger plans to bring about His chosen Servant.

The first of four poems, chapter 42 focuses on the character of the *servant*. This poem, also known as a 'Servant Song', describes the tasks of God's servant (verses 1–4) and then confirms them (verses 5–9). The functions of the Servant are listed clearly. We read that the servant will bring justice, suffer in silence, heal the sick, bring hope to those in need, remain steadfast, and establish justice throughout the earth. The description of the servant is stunning. God's Spirit would rest upon Him as He accomplished the tasks laid out in advance for Him to do. The servant would bring justice and righteousness to order. He would bring healing and help to people in need. As a silent servant, He would remain steadfast in His commitment and quiet in His suffering.

Today, we know this prophesied servant is Jesus. The Gospel of Matthew recounts this quote from Isaiah, acknowledging Jesus Christ as fulfilling this specific prophecy. *This was to fulfill what was spoken by the prophet Isaiah.* (Matthew 12:17) Jesus is the Suffering Servant who came to bring justice and healing to the world.

The significance of Isaiah 42 doesn't stop with the promise of a servant ruler, but more significantly, promises a new covenant for God's people.

> I will give you as a covenant for the people,
> a light for the nations.
>
> **ISAIAH 42:6**

Jesus Christ, as God's Servant, would establish a new covenant. Historically speaking, the covenant had been Israel's special privilege. God made covenants (solemn oaths) to His people throughout their history. Beginning initially under Noah, the covenant had been God's promise to draw His people back to Himself, redeem them, and bring them into a lifetime of freedom and obedience with Him. Continuing with Abram through the climax under Moses, God had extended covenants to His people for generations. Through each covenant promise, God would continue to manifest His goodness and grace by bringing His promises to fruition. God alone predicts and promises what's to come.

This newly referenced covenant would exist in the form of a servant. The context implies it would be a worldwide covenantal task—no longer just for the Israelites alone. He would bring the truth, heal personal disabilities, free captives, and transform circumstances to bring His people out of the darkness. The light would break through to establish a new, perfectly just order for the Lord to reign. God's Spirit would rest on the servant, again bringing God's presence down among the people.

Verses 2 and 3 introduce the quintessential Servant. Jesus Christ perfectly walked out His calling with a heart of faithful service. From His birth in a lowly manger to His ministry outreaches, Jesus constantly broke down expectations of how He would establish His kingdom. He was born in an unsuspecting manger because the inn had no more room.

He worked as a carpenter with His dad until He turned 30 years old. He grew up in Nazareth, not in a palace. He spoke with lepers and sat with prostitutes. Jesus constantly broke stereotypes and expectations of what it meant to serve others. He also specifically instructed His followers on how they could honor God by serving others.

> But whoever would be great among you must be your servant,
> and whoever would be first among you must be your slave, even
> as the Son of Man came not to be served but to serve, and to
> give his life as a ransom for many.
>
> **MATTHEW 20:26-28**

Jesus is the ultimate servant. He perfectly served His Father by giving His life on our behalf. While we can't fully replicate Jesus's ability to serve others, He does call us to reproduce a similar type of service towards others. We can be servants of the Lord. Through His power, we can bring the light of truth, care for those in need, offer freedom to captives, and lead people out of darkness. **Behold God's Servant.** He's the reason we celebrate this Advent season. He humbled Himself and gave His life as a ransom for us. He gave it all so that we can have everything with Him.

REFLECTIONS

What does this reveal to us about God?

What verse or words stand out to you in a fresh way?

How does this make you long for the second advent?

"Fear not, for I have redeemed you; I have called you by name, you are mine. When you pass through the waters, I will be with you; and through the rivers, they shall not overwhelm you; when you walk through fire you shall not be burned, and the flame shall not consume you."

ISAIAH 43:1-2

Precious in His Eyes

Read: Isaiah 43:1–7

Whether you're a fan of romantic comedies or not, under the surface, we all tend to love a good romance. We can't scroll through Netflix or Prime Video without seeing the latest new reality TV shows on dating or marriage. We root for strangers to find love, hoping they can experience the joy of being deeply known and truly loved.

Isaiah 43 is a personal love letter to God's people. Through the voice of Isaiah, God makes a list of promises to the Israelites. In verses 1–7, God says:

"I have redeemed you"
"I have called you by name"
"You are mine"
"I will be with you"
"You are precious in my eyes"
"[You are] honored"
"I love you"
"I give men in return for you"
"I created [you] for my glory"
"I formed and made [you]"

God's love oozes from these words. The God of the universe was telling His very sinful and disobedient people that He still loved them. No matter how far they'd gone, He knew them by name. No matter how much they'd disobeyed, He still loved them. He created them. He was with them. He would rescue them. Despite their sin, they were still God's *beloved* people.

God says the words *'I love you'* in verse 4. *Because you are precious in my eyes, and honored, and **I love you**...*(emphasis by author) The words 'precious,' 'honored,' and 'love' are written here in the perfect tense indicating that the past continues into the present. God still loved them, and He continues to love them. His love is ongoing because God is love.

With all the judgment and destruction in the first half of Isaiah, it can be possible to miss that God is loving. Yet, love compels God to seek after and restore the Israelites. Even when they were lost, and in rebellion, God loved them so much that He went after them to bring them back.

While the Bible is written for us, not everything is written to us. In short, the exact words God spoke to the Israelites do not always apply to us today. But the good news is that these very same promises given to God's people thousands of years ago are still true for us today. He has made a new promise, a new covenant, by sending His son Jesus as our Redeemer. Like God rescued the Israelites from exile, Jesus rescues and redeems those of us who choose to put our faith and trust in Him.

As believers, we too, are God's chosen people. These very same promises are for you. God has redeemed you. He knows you by name. You are His. He will be with you. You are precious in His eyes. You are honored by Him. He loves you. He gave His son for you. He created you for His glory. This love letter written thousands of years ago can also be for you.

At its very core, Isaiah 43 is a love song between an ancient people and their God, a God who lives and loves them in return. Just like the disobedient and sinful people in exile, God still sings songs rejoicing over you today. He lives, and He loves you still. Even when it seems like He is silent, God is still there. He's still reigning as our God. He knows you by name and hears your prayers.

If you feel like He doesn't hear you, has left you, or doesn't love you, take heart in these verses. Soak in their truth. Sit at His feet. The Creator of the universe who designed you still loves you and wants to walk with you today.

God loves you so much that He would send His only son, Jesus, to give up His own life so we can experience the most extraordinary love story of all time. In the second advent, these words can remind us that God's love still overflows for us today. We are deeply known and truly loved by our Heavenly Father. His love will never let us go.

REFLECTIONS

What does this reveal to us about God?

What verse or words stand out to you in a fresh way?

How does this make you long for the second advent?

"For I will pour
water on the thirsty
land, and streams
on the dry ground;
I will pour my Spirit
upon your offspring,
and my blessing on
your descendants."

ISAIAH 44:3

A Chosen People

Read: Isaiah 44:1–5

The Israelites had been living in exile for many years. The older generations of grandparents passed away, and new babies were born. Jewish holidays came and went. Like so many refugees today, the Israelites had rebuilt their lives in a new nation after enduring a tragedy. Weeks passed, then months, then years. God's silence must have felt deafening. The waiting must have felt agonizing. Where was God? These were His *chosen* people. *"Israel whom I have chosen!"* (Isaiah 44:1) But He remained silent.

God would not remain silent forever. He was (and still is) committed to His promises. He would come to rescue the Israelites from Babylon and lead them home to Jerusalem. His chosen people weren't lost, and He wasn't missing. God was still faithful to bring His promise to fruition. Despite their continual sin and disobedience, He would not forget them. He would lavish undeserved grace upon them. They were still His chosen, beloved bride.

A hint of a new promise subtly enters verse 3. God would pour out His Spirit on their offspring. For generations, He would bless their descendants.

> "For I will pour water on the thirsty land, and streams on the dry ground; I will pour my Spirit upon your offspring, and my blessing on your descendants."
>
> **ISAIAH 44:3**

It would be easy to breeze on by this promise in our context today without realizing the fullness of what Isaiah was prophesying. God was going to pour out His very own Spirit on His people. The same God who created and authored all things would send His personal Spirit to bless their descendants.

Today, as believers, we read this with a new lens after Jesus's life and ministry. We can see that the ministry and work of the Holy Spirit are being foretold here to the Israelites. Ephesians 1:13 tells us, *In him you also, when you heard the word of truth, the gospel of your salvation, and believed in him, were sealed with the promised Holy Spirit.* When we believe in Jesus and repent of our sins, we receive the Holy Spirit. This is God's special blessing and sign for us under the new covenant.

Even though we read about the work of the Spirit with new understanding, the Israelites, especially those in the generation of the Babylonian exile, would never have experienced God's tangible, personal presence in that way. They didn't have the language 'Holy Spirit' or the experience we have today through the empowerment of the Spirit as believers. Within the Old Testament and specifically the book of Isaiah, the Holy Spirit had only rested and filled select people that God had appointed with a specific task and purpose to bring His kingdom forward.

The Israelites would not have experienced God's presence. And that's the beauty of this promise here in verse 3. Something greater was coming. It was wilder than they could have possibly imagined. God was promising the future arrival of the Holy Spirit. His Spirit would bring blessings to the people and revive creation. The thirsty ground would have water. The grass would grow, and plants would flourish.

People of all tribes, tongues, and languages would enter this new kingdom. The good news would be available to the entire world. You could become part of God's family regardless of your historical, cultural, ethical, or social background. Throughout the world, God's people would come to celebrate and worship Him.

While we have a great promise in the days ahead, we still have to wait today. Our experiences often whisper that we can't live like this anymore. We dream of ways to escape our present realities. Life is too hard. It's not fair. People are crazy. There's too much suffering. Everything feels out of control. This isn't how it's supposed to be.

We can choose between two different attitudes as we wrestle with these daily struggles. We can believe that God has abandoned and punished us through His silence. Or we can choose to remember God's faithfulness to fulfill His word for thousands of years. God was faithful to bring the Israelites out of Babylon. Jesus is devoted to rescuing us from our sins. The Holy Spirit faithfully allows us to experience God's presence within us today.

He is faithful, even in the silence, unanswered prayers, and amidst terrible suffering. When we look at God's grace in our lives, we see He has been faithful to us. His words are trustworthy and true. He will remain loyal to His chosen people until He calls us home.

REFLECTIONS

What does this reveal to us about God?

What verse or words stand out to you in a fresh way?

How does this make you long for the second advent?

"I will make you as a light for the nations, that my salvation may reach to the end of the earth."

ISAIAH 49:6

Light for the Nations

Read: Isaiah 49:1–7

At long last, the Servant speaks. No longer do we hear His message in the third person. His voice sings aloud in song. *"The LORD **called me**..."* (Isaiah 49:1, emphasis by the author) The faithful servant, also called "Israel," describes who He will be. He is coming not just to do the things necessary for salvation but also to be the fulfillment of salvation for God's people.

The Servant would be a preacher of the Word. He would conquer by proclaiming the good news of the kingdom. His words would be pointed and fixed on the truth. They would build up and protect God's Word. The imagery in verse 2 compares a sharp sword and polished arrow with the effectiveness of God's Word.

A polished arrow is perfectly smooth because it's sanded down. Any unevenness could cause it to deflect in flight and ruin its accuracy. Like the arrow, God's Word is perfect. It's accurate and smooth, flawless and true. The arrow hits distant targets, not just ones nearby. It's reserved for a specific, chosen target, His people. It's not just for those close by, in this case, the Israelites, but for people from every tribe, tongue, and language. It's universal.

The sword wins battles close at hand. A sword fight is face-to-face combat. God's Word is personal, like an intense one-on-one battle with a sword. It provides protection and a covering of truth.

For the word of God is living and active, sharper than any two-edged sword, piercing to the division of soul and of spirit, of joints and of marrow, and discerning the thoughts and intentions of the heart.

HEBREWS 4:12

God's Word is still living and active today. Thousands of years later, we're still reading the same story. His Word pierces the hardest hearts and captures the greatest of sinners. It speaks to humans and instructs the divine.

The Servant would bring God's Word to life. He fulfills God's plan not only through His actions but also through His life. He is the living Word. The Servant doesn't just oversee the saving of God's people; He is the salvation for the people. Isaiah foresaw a servant with an actual human nature who proved to be the fulfillment of God's promise.

Jesus is the very person that the world needs. He came to bring the good news for all of us. As the Servant, He brings the gospel to the nations. No longer is the good news just for the people of Israel. It is for those all over the world. His words are proclaimed throughout the world to call others close to Him. He transforms hearts. He brings His very presence. He is a new light for the nations.

God's Word came to dwell with the Servant in the person of Jesus. The Servant would be a light for the nations. Jesus's life and ministry bring kingdom light to the earth. This light illuminates the global Church. Like a bride glowing on her wedding day, the bride of Christ is radiant with God's presence. God's Word continues to bring light to us. His Word is universal—for the edification of all believers, but it's also uniquely personal. God speaks to us through His Word and His Spirit. We can access this same Word by reading Scripture and talking with Him. His Word illuminates our path and gives us the wisdom to walk in the light.

We can hold on to this great hope in the darkest months of the year. A new dawn is still coming. We can look back and see glimpses of the light breaking through. Our Servant was born in great darkness, yet He came to establish a kingdom of light. He's made a way for us to go from death to life. We can put our hope in Him as the light to come.

"In the bleak mid-winter
All creation groans,
For a world in darkness
Frozen like a stone
Light is breaking, in a stable for a throne."
He Shall Reign Forevermore by Chris Tomlin

REFLECTIONS

What does this reveal to us about God?

What verse or words stand out to you in a fresh way?

How does this make you long for the second advent?

But he was pierced for
our transgressions; he
was crushed for our
iniquities; upon him
was the chastisement
that brought us peace,
and with his wounds
we are healed.

ISAIAH 53:5

The Suffering Servant

Read: Isaiah 52:13–53:12

The night has been dark, but a sunrise is slowly lifting over the horizon. It's the dawn of redemption—a thrill of hope. God makes a way for the Israelites once again. He leads them out of exile and guides them back to their home in Jerusalem. The time of their salvation was drawing near.

From the great homecoming, we turn to see the solitary Person whose suffering and agony would make it all possible. Isaiah 52–53 gives one of the most explicit pictures of the coming Messiah. The Servant would accomplish salvation for God's people, but it would come at a significant cost. He would be despised and rejected. Everyone would abandon Him. He would suffer and die for the people's sins, paying the ultimate price.

This beautiful poem begins and ends with hopeful celebration. It starts with the end of the story. One day, God would crown the Servant with honor and glory. The Servant would be exalted and lifted up. Knowing the final outcome allows us to read the prophecy with hopeful eyes instead of desperate despair. The Servant would overcome the darkness, and God would enthrone Him on high. More than a tragic tale, this is an epic story of hope.

The Servant would suffer. He would experience unimaginable physical and emotional pain. *His appearance was so marred, beyond human semblance.* (Isaiah 52:14) His body would be physically assaulted. He would be so scarred from His suffering that He would no longer be recognizable. He would experience physical pain and undergo deep emotional turmoil. *He was despised and rejected by men.* (Isaiah 53:3) All of His friends and family would desert Him. He would feel profound rejection. He was to be despised and hated by people who didn't even know Him.

> He was oppressed, and he was afflicted, yet he opened not his
> mouth; like a lamb that is led to the slaughter,
> and like a sheep that before its shearers is silent,
> so he opened not his mouth.
>
> **ISAIAH 53:7**

The Servant would remain silent amidst the accusations and lies, steadfast in His mission. The Suffering Servant would willingly participate in an agonizing betrayal. He would withhold His words and not fight back against His oppressors. The Servant wouldn't argue His case. Instead, He would willingly lay down His life. He would knowingly sacrifice Himself as part of God's grand plan for the redemption of His people.

Behold, Jesus Christ, the Suffering Servant, was coming. He wouldn't arrive on a throne or through noble birth. His origins were of the most humble beginning. He was born in an unremarkable manger, likely in a hillside cave or courtyard alongside the animals. The holy seed had come to Bethlehem. *Like a root out of dry ground* (Isaiah 53:2), Jesus arrived in the most unassuming place.

Jesus lived on mission to redeem humankind and bring the kingdom to earth. He knew the bigger story. Jesus paid the price for our sins so that we no longer have to offer our own sacrifices for our sins. He became our sacrifice as part of God's grand plan to restore His people.

> Out of the anguish of his soul he shall see and be satisfied; by his
> knowledge shall the righteous one, my servant,
> make many to be accounted righteous, and he shall
> bear their iniquities.
>
> **ISAIAH 53:11**

Through His sacrifice, the Servant made us righteous before God. We are now declared a holy people. Righteousness is not something we can accomplish for ourselves. Christ secured our righteousness for us with His finishing work on the cross. He poured out His soul, even to death so that we can stand in perfect freedom before the final Judge.

The Suffering Servant came to lay His life down for us. Though He was like an innocent lamb, He withstood rejection, judgment, and physical torture to cleanse us of our sins. He paid the price. Today, we are free through His finished work on the cross on our behalf. Is there a better Christmas gift? Jesus Christ came for *us*.

REFLECTIONS

What does this reveal to us about God?

What verse or words stand out to you in a fresh way?

How does this make you long for the second advent?

"Come, everyone who thirsts, come to the waters; and he who has no money, come, buy and eat! Come, buy wine and milk without money and without price."

ISAIAH 55:1

Come to Him

Read: Isaiah 55:1-13

Over and over again, the Israelites break their promises to God. They forget His faithfulness. They don't remember His provision. They lose their faith and put their trust in something else that can't hold its weight. Yet despite their faithlessness, over and over again, we see God offer compassion to His people.

The Israelites' story is one with consistent patterns. The people rebel, God gets angry, there is an intercession, God relents from His anger, and there are consequences for their sins. Throughout their history, the Israelites continued to fall into this pattern and desperately needed covering for their sins.

Similarly, we too, fall into these same patterns today. Like the Israelites, we see patterns of discontentment and jealousy still rampant in our lives. Whether conscious or subconscious, we rebel against God. Even though God is displeased with our disobedience and rebellion, Jesus has already paid the price of our sins.

We are people in desperate need of unrelenting mercy, yet despite our failures, our God is a God of overflowing compassion. He continually pours out grace for us. God preserves the Church through a continual pattern of unrelenting grace. The compassion of the Lord never fails us.

The steadfast love of the Lord never ceases; his mercies never
come to an end; they are new every morning;
great is your faithfulness.

LAMENTATIONS 3:22–23

His love and mercy never cease. Isaiah 55 is a gospel message. It's a
passionate appeal to the thirsty and wicked. God offers us a free gift of
compassion when we believe in Him and repent of our sins. There is still
time to receive this gift. He says—

"Come, everyone who thirsts"
"Come to the waters"
"Come, buy and eat"
"Come, buy wine and milk"
"Without money and without price"

Paraphrased from ISAIAH 55:1–2

He supplies the water for the thirsty. He gives away these gifts for free.
There is no cost—poverty is no longer a barrier. We can eat as we need.
There is still a purchase and a price, but He has already paid that on our
behalf. This feast is one of love and forgiveness. It's the washing of fresh
grace and mercy. There is refreshment in the water, joy in the wine, and
richness in the milk. The language is figurative for God's salvation with
the Servant at its core.

The call is both singular and plural. The invitation to come is plural
and inclusive. We are all invited to gather around this feast. It's an open
call to the people. God is casting a bigger invitation for His kingdom. His
grace is available for everyone who turns to Him. But it's also intentionally
personal. If you are thirsty, this food and drink is for you. "*Delight yourselves
in rich food*" (Isaiah 55:2) that He has prepared for you. God is extending
His compassion specifically to you.

> "Seek the LORD while he may be found; call upon him
> while he is near...let him return to the LORD, that he
> may have compassion on him, and to our God,
> for he will abundantly pardon."

ISAIAH 55:6–7

Seek the Lord. Return to Him. His compassion is abundant, and His mercy is new every morning. Sing praises to His name. Extend the invitation to call others to the table. Savor the banquet feast. Continue to seek the Lord. He welcomes sinners with open arms. His grace is more than we can ever comprehend.

We remember God's faithfulness and compassion that Jesus came to allow us to enjoy this banquet feast while we were still sinners. His grace is new every morning for us. As we slow down and savor this season of Advent, we come to Him. We come because we're thirsty. We come because we're hungry. We come because we are spiritually poor. He will give us a fresh filling of His abundant compassion. He will fill us with His grace and mercy so that we can be His kingdom light.

REFLECTIONS

What does this reveal to us about God?

What verse or words stand out to you in a fresh way?

How does this make you long for the second advent?

Thus says the LORD:
"Keep justice, and
do righteousness, for
soon my salvation
will come, and my
righteousness be
revealed."

ISAIAH 56:1

A Waiting People

Read: Isaiah 56:1–8

At long last, the Israelites had returned home from exile to Jerusalem. They were finally free. God had brought His people back home from Babylon through Cyrus the Great, the new king of Persia. After so many long years in exile, they returned with a mission to rebuild the temple and re-establish their city. They were finally home after so many years of longing and hoping for someone to rescue them.

The setting shifts from Babylon back to the city of Jerusalem in Isaiah 56 as the book transitions to its final section. God had worked through Cyrus the Great to save and rescue them from captivity. Their arrival home should've been the grand finale and resolution to the Israelites' story. They had been redeemed and restored, but something was still missing.

What we see throughout the last few chapters of Isaiah is a people who are still waiting. After decades in exile, the Israelites believed their waiting was finally over. Their deep desire to return home had come to fruition. Families should have rejoiced and begun collectively rebuilding the city to restore it from its war-torn days. However, upon re-entering the city, we see that many of their needs were still unsatisfied. They were still living in a broken world. People were still choosing to live in rebellion. Even though they were home, it wasn't a city of perfect peace, justice, and righteousness. Conflict and frustration began to rise once more.

While they'd been rescued and were hopeful to rebuild and restore Jerusalem, we see in the final chapters that people still long for a home in this broken world. The Israelites weren't in their eternal home quite yet. Their deepest needs and longings couldn't be satisfied here on earth. Their hope for a restored home and dwelling place with God was longing for heaven and a perfect world where God will rule and dwell with His people.

Much like the Israelites in this final section, we also feel the same longing for home. We work hard to create places that feel like 'home' for us to live in. We dream about bigger houses, new furniture, and better cars. We think about future seasons and the things they could offer us that we don't have quite yet. Whether it's a new kitchen table, couch, or art for the walls, we are constantly working to make ourselves feel more at home, even when it can never fully live up to that expectation.

Isaiah 56:1 sets the scene for the Israelites on their return. God says, *"Keep justice, and do righteousness, for soon my salvation **will** come..."* His promise for their salvation still stood. Their return to Jerusalem wasn't actually the end of their story. God was promising to bring ultimate salvation. Their home wasn't permanent. It wasn't on earth. It was actually in heaven.

The first eight verses of Isaiah 56 depict a grand picture of God's kingdom in heaven. The invitation to join God's family would no longer only be for the Israelites, it would also be for the foreigners. God extends His invitation to the outsider. He would send a savior not just to rescue the Israelites out of Babylon but also to rescue all of His people throughout the entire world.

God was coming to rescue the foreigner. He was coming for those who felt like they had no home. He was coming for the refugee. He was coming for the restless, the homeless, and the weary traveler. His promises for a Savior were so much bigger than just one nation at this single period in time. God was coming to make a way for people all throughout the world, for centuries to come, to be rescued and brought home to Him.

Isaiah 56:1 is precisely where the Church still stands today. We look back towards the cross and remember Jesus, *our Savior*. And we look forward in anticipation, awaiting the final divine act where Jesus will return to rescue His people from our rebellion once again. He is coming back. The Church will be rescued and restored. Our Savior is coming. All over the world, believers wait in this same anticipation. We wait for the promised return of King Jesus, our Anointed Conqueror.

Today, we hold on to this treasured hope. We only experience this hope within the waiting. A hope that (although it might dwindle at times) never ceases to exist for us. A hope that prays and sits in expectation of what's yet to come. We know that a better home, city, and earth is coming. Together, the global Church awaits this glorious day. Jesus will return for His bride, the Church. His salvation is coming.

REFLECTIONS

What does this reveal to us about God?

What verse or words stand out to you in a fresh way?

How does this make you long for the second advent?

Your sun shall no
more go down,
nor your moon
withdraw itself; for
the LORD will be
your everlasting
light, and your days
of mourning shall
be ended.

ISAIAH 60:20

The Light of Glory

Read: Isaiah 60:1–22

A revival is coming. Isaiah 60 paints the glorious picture of the restored city of Jerusalem at the consummation. The vision is magnificent. Yahweh has brought His full glory down to a restored earth. He visibly dwells on Zion (Jerusalem), with His glory shining so bright that the world no longer needs its light from the sun. People flock to the city, drawn to the presence of the light.

God's people radiate His glory in the light. They are finally a restored creation! Inwardly and outwardly, they are shining, new beings. The vision unfolds with a tremendous homeward march. Men, women, and children head to Zion from every corner of the earth. People travel from distant places on boats, with babies, and carrying gifts.

It's the ultimate pilgrimage home. Faithful servants and believers from all over the world travel to gather in the city where God dwells. His presence draws them from near and far. King Jesus reigns as His followers come together at last. The kingdom has finally fully come.

People from all nations proclaim the gospel's good news as they come. They bring offerings and tributes to the Lord with gold, frankincense, and wealth. The city gates are continuously open because people keep arriving with gifts. Day and night, kings and subjects alike stream through the city gates towards the glory of the Lord.

King Jesus meets all worldly desires. The people are finally home. They are at rest. The deepest desires of their hearts are not just completed but overwhelmed by the goodness of God. In the sky, on the land, and through the sea, humankind and creation approach the restored city of Zion.

Isaiah 60 describes a similar new Jerusalem to what we see in Revelation 21.

> And I saw no temple in the city, for its temple is the Lord God the Almighty and the Lamb. And the city has no need of sun or moon to shine on it, for the glory of God gives it light, and its lamp is the Lamb. By its light will the nations walk, and the kings of the earth will bring their glory into it.
>
> **REVELATIONS 21:22–24**

Revelation describes the city of Jerusalem as a rare jewel, clear as crystal, with pure gold. Jewels adorn every part of the city with streets of gold like transparent glass. God's glory shines its bright light, illuminating the city with His holy presence. Both Isaiah and John describe the city with unparalleled splendor. The imagery is stark, with vibrant images of luxury and wealth that are almost unbelievable for us to imagine.

The visions in Isaiah and Revelation of the restored city focus on God's constant presence. God dwells amidst the people. He no longer lives in a tabernacle, temple, or human heart. Like the original Garden of Eden, God inhabits the restored creation with humanity. Everyone who comes to experience Zion gets to have personal and intimate knowledge of Him. No longer is there a sin separation that keeps His people from His presence. Everyone and everything will be made new.

One day, this prophetic vision will come true. King Jesus will return. The world will be new. Justice and righteousness will reign. After the grand conquest over darkness, God will return to dwell on a restored earth. A grand pilgrimage will occur as people from every tribe, tongue, and language draw near to see and experience God's presence on earth.

This vision gives us hope because the Light of the world has already come. In John 8:12, Jesus told the people, *"I am the light of the world. Whoever follows me will not walk in darkness, but will have the light of life."* Jesus has brought the kingdom light to earth. When we follow him, we receive the light of life. We get to taste and sample the beauty of God's Spirit in what's to come.

As our candles flicker on a dark winter night, it reminds us that the light of the world has already come. The flame may flicker, but it can never be put out. The light will win over the darkness. The kingdom light has come, and He is coming back to light the world ablaze with His glory. We get to fix our gaze upon the Light in great anticipation of the divine restoration yet to come.

REFLECTIONS

What does this reveal to us about God?

What verse or words stand out to you in a fresh way?

How does this make you long for the second advent?

I will greatly rejoice in
the LORD; my soul shall
exult in my God, for he
has clothed me with the
garments of salvation; he
has covered me with the
robe of righteousness,
as a bridegroom decks
himself like a priest with
a beautiful headdress, and
as a bride adorns herself
with her jewels.

ISAIAH 61:10

The Bride of Christ

Read: Isaiah 61:1–11

Following this grand vision, the Anointed Servant speaks again. The Spirit of the Lord is upon Him. He has come to bring good news to the poor and heal the brokenhearted. The good news has finally reached its culmination. The Servant recounts all the promised blessings that will come true through the restored creation.

All of the sadness, pain, and suffering has passed away. Instead of sorrow, praise fills their spirits. Places that experienced destruction are rebuilt. People are restored with exceeding joy. God has transformed the pain points from former suffering with their perfect remedy. Instead of ashes for mourning formerly smeared across the forehead, beautiful headdresses take their place. The oil of gladness replaces the ashes for mourning. This description is subtle but encouraging for us to realize God's specific intentionality in the restoration.

In ancient times, royalty used this ceremonial expression for times of excessive celebration. The oil of gladness symbolizes joy and rejoicing. In this prophecy, the Anointed One replaces sorrow with joy. The special oil is not just for royalty and leaders but all who have mourned. The people's status had changed. They are fully restored. They are now *"oaks of righteousness"* (Isaiah 61:3) because God has personally recovered, transported, and replanted them into His garden. Their new status as righteous people stood because God did the work to bring them out of their former place and replant them with Him. Once again, it is a divine display of His glory and restoration.

Isaiah looks forward to the final consummation, where only God's chosen people would inhabit the restored world. Yet what Isaiah saw has already begun to be experienced today in the Church. Verses 5-9 shine a light on the people of God. They would stand out from among the nations. Foreigners would desire to join them. In God's glory, they would boast. Instead of shame, they would find freedom and joy. Their children would be called blessed.

Through the work of the Holy Spirit, believers are remade through the power of the Spirit and the working of the Word to become more like Christ. As we become more transformed into His likeness, we become more distinct and set apart. In between the advents, we can experience some of these promised blessings for the future restored world. We get to pursue justice for our neighbors. We have the opportunity to choose joy amidst suffering. We have the privilege to care for others who are hurting around us. The body of Christ can exude the peace, hope, love, and joy only found through His ongoing work.

The Church, the entire body of believers, prepares itself as the bride of Christ. This picture reveals a divine preparation that is already happening. The wedding imagery gives us a glimpse of the coming promise of commitment between Christ, the bridegroom, and the Church, His bride. The bride is getting ready. She is actively getting dressed, putting on her jewelry, adorning herself with beauty, and preparing to meet her groom. The Church awaits His coming arrival. In the waiting, the anticipation rises. He will be arriving soon.

In Luke 4, Jesus teaches for the very first time. In His hometown of Nazareth, He stands to read aloud in the synagogue. He opens the scroll to Isaiah 61 and proceeds to read this passage. Jesus begins His ministry with these exact words. After reading, he rolled up the scroll and sat back down with all eyes fixed on Him.

And he began to say to them, "Today this Scripture has been fulfilled in your hearing."

LUKE 4:21

The same words that we read today were read aloud by Jesus thousands of years ago to announce the arrival of His kingdom. Jesus came as the Anointed Servant to bring good news for all who would receive and believe it. He healed the sick, forgave the sinner, and freed the oppressed. His kingdom has been proclaimed throughout history. His people are set apart, shining with His promised Spirit, a light for all to see. He came to make way for his bride, and He's coming back for her. In this, we greatly rejoice. He alone has brought us our salvation and is coming back for us.

This good news is for us today. Jesus is coming back as our groom. We await the glorious day of the wedding feast when He will return to commit Himself to us forever as His bride. Our ashes will be remade into celebratory oil. Every part of our brokenness and sadness will be restored through His intentional care *uniquely* for us. He is coming to make all things new for you. Your groom is coming. Together, we await this glorious hope

REFLECTIONS

What does this reveal to us about God?

What verse or words stand out to you in a fresh way?

How does this make you long for the second advent?

"For behold, I create new heavens and a new earth, and the former things shall not be remembered or come into mind."

ISAIAH 65:17

A New Home

Read: Isaiah 65:17–25

Much like these final chapters of Isaiah, we long for the wrestling between good and evil to end. When Jesus returns as the Anointed Conqueror, He will bring His kingdom to its fullness. As part of the final act, the entirety of the universe will be made new. The created order, like day and night, will no longer be needed. We will no longer remember former broken things.

While it's challenging to think about losing some sweet memories from this life, God follows this statement with a call for emphatic joy.

> "But be glad and rejoice forever in that which I create;
> for behold, I create Jerusalem to be a joy."
>
> **ISAIAH 65:18**

Without sin, pain, and suffering, only joy abounds. There is nothing to fear. We can have blissful delight without any awareness of our former sins and suffering.

God describes the restored world with a list of hardships that will no longer exist after the final restoration. There will be no more weeping or distress. Infants will no longer pass away. People will live to an older age. Death will no longer be a threat. Grief will no longer be possible.

We will rebuild houses and inhabit them. We will work the land and see the fruit of our labor. There will be no stealing or impartiality. Everything will be fair and just. We will toil and enjoy the work of our hands. Our work will be purposeful. We won't have to live in fear for our lives or our children's lives. God will be with our offspring and descendants. He will answer our call before we even begin to speak. There will be no more danger. There will be no more hurt or destruction in our eternal home.

The picture of the new heavens and new earth isn't one of angels lounging around playing harps on floating clouds. It's not one of our spirits floating around some celestial palace. It's interesting here that everything Isaiah describes is something from our 'old' world where we live today. Nothing new is introduced (no new creatures, buildings, etc.). We can picture everything that he describes here.

This vivid description in Isaiah 65 is our forever home. It should be a familiar setting for us. It's a place where we get to dwell in perfection with God *and also* live, work, have families, and enjoy the work of our hands. His Word tells us that we get to participate in cultivating our restored world. This restorative work is a guarantee. We get to rebuild buildings and create things that bring life and flourishing to our city.

It's the perfect life that we can't experience in our earthly home today. We will have security without fear of death or unexpected tragedy. We will have deep fulfillment in our work and labor. We will have peace and the presence of God. He will exceed every bit of our deepest longings as we experience love and joy firsthand in its fullness.

This is the good news for us in the waiting. As God's chosen people, we get to live in this restored creation! Isaiah prophesies an incredible picture of what our future will hold. We get to experience the best parts of life without the brokenness of sin. It's more than just a place with no sadness or suffering; it will be a world full of opportunity for creation and cultivation. The excitement of what's to come should be good news for our weary souls. We are promised a perfectly restored universe with our God.

The fulfillment of this prophecy for the new heavens and earth awaits Christ's second coming. 2 Peter 3:13 reiterates this promise.

> But according to his promise we are waiting for new heavens and a new earth in which righteousness dwells.

We are waiting, have been waiting, and will continue to wait until Jesus returns in His perfect timing. In the meantime, we have the opportunity to experience part of this future blessing through our faith. We get to participate in bringing justice, peace, love, and hope to our world. As believers, we can obey God's commands to bring glory and honor to Him. We get to become the light that the whole world sees.

This Christmas season, we have a fresh reminder that this is not our forever home. No house, land, or city can ever fully meet our desires in this life. But there are good tidings of great joy for this Advent. A new home is coming. Jesus is coming back to bring His kingdom to earth. There will be new heavens and earth for our stewardship.

Hope has a name, and His name is Jesus. As we slow down to celebrate His birth and life, we fix our eyes on Him. He gives us what we need to put our faith and hope in Him. *Behold*, we wait together with expectant joy for when our King returns.

REFLECTIONS

What does this reveal to us about God?

What verse or words stand out to you in a fresh way?

How does this make you long for the second advent?

All this took place to fulfill what the Lord had spoken by the prophet: "Behold, the virgin shall conceive and bear a son, and they shall call his name Immanuel" (which means, God with us).

MATTHEW 1:22-23

Our King is Born

Read: Matthew 1:18–25

Jesus Christ was born in a primitive stable. *And she gave birth to her firstborn son and wrapped him in swaddling cloths and laid him in a manger, because there was no place for them in the inn.* (Luke 2:7) The angel of the Lord appeared to the shepherds, keeping watch over their flock that night. With a grand proclamation, an angel announced the long-awaited Messiah had finally come. (Luke 2:10-11)

The heavens and earth rejoiced! A multitude of the heavenly host appeared and began praising God, singing *"Glory to God in the highest, and on earth peace among those with whom he is pleased!"* (Luke 2:14) An army of angels sang and proclaimed His arrival. The glory of the Lord shone brightly over the dark night. *Immanuel,* God with us, had come to earth in a humble manger. The world would never be the same. God had sent His son to deliver His people.

Jesus came as the Messianic King. *Yeshua,* Jesus's personal name, means 'Yahweh saves.' Jesus had come to rescue God's people and save us from our sins. He was the promised holy seed. His earthly life would establish eternal life for all believers. He came to rule and bring about God's eternal kingdom *for us.*

As the Messianic King, Jesus brought His rule and reign to earth. He gives us wisdom as the Wonderful Counselor. He protects us as Mighty

God. He is divine and eternal, an Everlasting Father to lovingly guide us. Jesus brings heavenly peace to the earth as the Prince of Peace.

> For to us a child is born, to us a son is given; and the government shall be upon his shoulder, and his name shall be called Wonderful Counselor, Mighty God, Everlasting Father, Prince of Peace.
>
> **ISAIAH 9:6**

Jesus came as our Suffering Servant. His life began as an embodiment of His humility for us. Born in a manger, He had no royal treatment or grand entrance. Only His parents, some shepherds, a few wise men, and close family recognized He was born.

But God knew. He had made a plan to redeem humanity from their sin. Jesus would humble Himself to the lowest position as our Suffering Servant. He lived the perfect life we couldn't live and suffered for us so that He could be the necessary atonement for our sins. He willingly came to earth to be fully human and man as part of God's perfect plan for salvation. Jesus gave His life as a ransom for our sins.

> He was oppressed, and he was afflicted, yet he opened not his mouth; like a lamb that is led to the slaughter, and like a sheep that before its shearers is silent, so he opened not his mouth.
>
> **ISAIAH 53:7**

Jesus came as the Anointed Conquerer. He made a way for us when there was no way. If we believe in Him and repent of our sins, we will have everlasting life. God chose and anointed Jesus to be the messenger to deliver His people. He came to break the curse of sin and death. Jesus has already won the battle. He has conquered death on our behalf.

The Spirit of the Lord GOD is upon me, because the LORD has anointed me to bring good news to the poor; he has sent me to bind up the brokenhearted, to proclaim liberty to the captives, and the opening of the prison to those who are bound.

ISAIAH 61:1

Jesus is our greatest gift. This is the best news for us on Christmas morning. He has come as our King. He lived a perfect life and endured tremendous suffering on our behalf as the Suffering Servant. And He has established God's kingdom as the Anointed Conquerer. The light is breaking through the darkness. Jesus has brought God's kingdom down to earth. The light has come, and it will never be overcome.

The good news is our hope during Advent: Jesus has come. We remember His birth, life, ministry, and sacrifice, all gifts for us. We reread the story of His birth and remember His promises to us. Looking back at His faithfulness gives us hope for what's yet to come.

Jesus was born to rescue you. He came to bring you hope on the darkest night. Jesus is coming back to establish a permanent home for you. He's faithfully with you until the end of time.

He is the greatest gift you'll ever receive.

REFLECTIONS

What does this reveal to us about God?

What verse or words stand out to you in a fresh way?

How does this make you long for the second advent?

And the angel said to them,

"Fear not, for behold, I bring

you good news of great joy that

will be for all the people.

For unto you is born this day

in the city of David a Savior,

who is Christ the Lord."

LUKE 2:10–11

Notes

1 Goldstick, Jason E., Rebecca M. Cunningham, and Patrick M. Carter. 2022. "Current Causes of Death in Children and Adolescents in the United States." *New England Journal of Medicine* 386, no. April (April). https://doi.org/10.1056/nejmc2201761.

2 Cherry, Elliott. 2022. "A River Runs to It." Sermon. November 27. https://midtownfellowship.org/12-south/sermons/a-river-runs-to-it-isa-21-5/.

3 "Human Trafficking: The Third Largest Crime Industry in the World." 2018. ECPAT. August 6, 2018. https://ecpat.org/trafficking-the-third-largest-crime-industry-in-the-world/.

4 Harzog, Beverly. 2022. "How Many Americans Are Living Paycheck to Paycheck?" *U.S. News & World Report*, June 8, 2022. https://money.usnews.com/credit-cards/articles/how-many-americans-are-living-paycheck-to-paycheck.

5 Kramer, Stephanie, and Hackett. 2022. "Modeling the Future of Religion in America." https://www.pewresearch.org/religion/2022/09/13/modeling-the-future-of-religion-in-america/.

6 J. A. Motyer, *The Prophecy of Isaiah: An Introduction & Commentary* (Downers Grove, IL: InterVarsity Press, 1996), 493.

Made in the USA
Coppell, TX
01 December 2023

25102294R00066